This journal belongs to:

_____

I CAN MAKE A KICK ASS JOURNAL BUT
THE INTENTIONS YOU SET WHEN USING
IT ARE ALSO IMPORTANT.

FOR THIS JOURNAL, "I'M SETTING AN
INTENTION TO":

_____
_____
_____
_____

GRIEF F*CKING SUCKS

SIMONE EBRIGHT, MA
MENTY B'S PUBLISHING

INTRODUCTION

GRIEF F*CKING SUCKS.

I DON'T KNOW WHAT BROUGHT YOU TO THIS BOOK, BUT I KNOW IT IS WITH EMPATHY & LIFE EXPERIENCE THAT I WANT YOU TO KNOW YOU ARE NOT ALONE IN YOUR GRIEF.

LET'S START WITH **THE "DEFINITION" OF GRIEF** FROM OXFORD LANGUAGES: *"DEEP SORROW, ESPECIALLY THAT CAUSED BY SOMEONE'S DEATH"*. TO ME, **GRIEF IS SO MUCH MORE THAN DEEP SORROW**. IT IS A MONUMENTAL LOSS, IMPACTING ALL PARTS OF LIFE: SELF, LOVE, RELATIONSHIPS, WORK, PRODUCTIVITY, AND SO MUCH MORE.

WHEN WE GO THROUGH A LOSS, WE ARE NOT JUST LOSING THE PERSON, PET, OR INTERACTION THAT WE CARED FOR, WE ARE LOSING THE FUTURE ABILITY TO BE APART OF THAT AS WELL.

ASIDE FROM THE OVERWHELMING SHIFT IN OUR LIVES, GRIEF ALSO CHANGES THE WAY WE FUNCTION IN DAILY LIFE. IN AMERICAN CULTURE- THIS IS A BIG NO NO... WE ARE A WORKFORCE SOCIETY, SO WHEN YOU GO THROUGH A LOSS OR HARD LIFE TRANSITION IT CAN SOMETIMES FEEL LIKE THE WORLD IS SAYING: *GET IT TOGETHER- AND KEEP MOVING ON*, WHICH CAN FEEL INVALIDATING.

GRIEF IS ON YOUR TIMELINE. I'M NOT SAYING GO HIDE OUT IN YOUR BED UNTIL YOUR FRIENDS START GETTING CONCERNED, BUT I AM SAYING TO GIVE YOURSELF GRACE. GRACE TO GRIEVE WITHOUT STIPULATIONS. EAT THAT CUPCAKE, TAKE A DAY OFF, BUY *THIS* JOURNAL, GET YOUR SELF-CARE ON.

COPYRIGHT © 2021 SIMONE EBRIGHT
PUBLISHED IN THE UNITED STATES BY LULU
AND AMAZON
MENTY B'S PUBLISHING

ALL RIGHTS RESERVED. NO PART OF THIS BOOK
MAY BE REPRODUCED BY ANY MECHANICAL,
PHOTOGRAPHIC, OR ELECTRONIC PROCESS;
NOR MAY IT BE STORED IN A RETRIEVAL
SYSTEM, TRANSMITTED, OR OTHERWISE BE
COPIED FOR PUBLIC OR PRIVATE USE.

PAPERBACK ISBN: 978-0-578-32276-6
1ST EDITION, NOVEMBER 2021

PRINTED IN THE UNITED STATES OF AMERICA

IF YOU GET ANYTHING FROM THIS- ***REMEMBER YOUR GRIEF IS VALID****, YOU HAVE SUPPORT FROM LOVED ONES,* ***YOU HAVE THE POWER TO PROCESS YOUR FEELINGS*** *AND IF YOU WANT PROFESSIONAL SUPPORT YOU CAN FIND THERAPISTS IN YOUR LOCAL AREA.*

DISCLAIMER: THIS JOURNAL IS BASED ON PERSONAL EXPERIENCES AND THEREFOR CANNOT REPLACE MENTAL HEALTH OR MEDICAL SERVICES. PLEASE KEEP IN MIND THAT NO JOURNAL IS NOT A "CURE ALL" FOR GRIEF SYMPTOMS AND THAT ALL MENTAL HEALTH & LONG TERM GRIEF SYMPTOMS SHOULD BE ADDRESSED WITH A MENTAL HEALTH PROFESSIONAL.

THE AUTHOR SIMONE EBRIGHT, HAS A MASTER'S DEGREE IN COUPLES & FAMILY THERAPY AND HOLDS A CURRENT LMFTA LICENSE IN THE STATE OF WASHINGTON. THIS JOURNAL IS BASED ON HER PERSONAL EXPERIENCES WITH GRIEF & LOSS. USING THIS JOURNAL IS BASED ON THE READERS OWN DECISION-MAKING AND KOGER COUNSELING, PLLC & MENTY B'S PUBLISHING ARE NOT LIABLE FOR HOW YOU INTERPRET OR PERCEIVE ITS CONTENTS. THIS BOOK DOES NOT MEAN TO REPLACE ANY MEDICAL, OR MENTAL HEALTH ADVISE OR RESOURCES.

THIS JOURNAL IS WRITTEN IN A OPEN STYLE, SO YOU CAN OPEN UP TO ANY PAGE TO SELECT WHICH PROMPT YOU WANT TO FOCUS ON.

YOU CAN UTILIZE THE PROMPTS IN WHICHEVER ORDER YOU PREFER.

*This book is dedicated
to all the broken hearts.*

You are strong.

For the ones experiencing Grief

GRIEF F*CKING SUCKS.
THESE CHAPTERS GO THROUGH POTENTIAL DIFFERENT EXPERIENCES OF TYPES OF GRIEF- BUT IT IS ONLY THE SURFACE OF WHAT IS OUT THERE.
YOUR EXPERIENCES AND EMOTIONS ARE VALID.

IF YOU WANT SUPPORT FROM A THERAPIST GET IT! IT IS NEVER TOO EARLY OR TOO LATE TO MAKE A NEW CONNECTION.

**DESCRIBE THE PERSON YOU LOST:
WHAT WERE THEY LIKE?**

WHAT ARE SOME THINGS THEY LOVED?

WHAT IS A FUNNY MEMORY YOU HAVE OF THIS PERSON?

WHAT IS A MEMORY THAT MAKES YOU THINK "THAT TOTALLY DESCRIBES THEM"?

WHAT DO YOU MISS THE MOST?
(ABOUT THE PERSON, PET, RELATIONSHIP)

DOES IT FEEL SURREAL? *IF SO, THAT IS NORMAL. DEATH AND CHANGE CAN BE DISMANTLING. THIS BOOK IS YOURS TO PROCESS YOUR FEELINGS, BECAUSE* **NO TWO PEOPLE GRIEVE THE SAME WAY.**

WHAT HAS CHANGED IN YOUR LIFE DUE TO THIS GRIEF?

WHAT RITUALS CAN YOU ADD TO YOUR LIFE TO HONOR YOUR LOVED ONE(S) WHO ARE GONE? (THIS COULD BE WATCHING YOUR LOVED ONES FAVORITE MOVIE, LISTENING TO MUSIC THEY LOVED, ADDING PICTURES AROUND THE HOUSE- THERE ARE ENDLESS CREATIVE POSSIBILITIES)

**USE THIS PAGE TO DRAW OUT
SOME WAYS
TO HONOR YOUR LOVED ONE**

**WHO CAN YOU RELY ON
FOR EMOTIONAL SUPPORT?**

**WHO CAN YOU RELY ON FOR
SOME FUN?**

**WHO CAN YOU RELY ON FOR WHEN
YOU ARE IN A CRISIS?**

WHAT EMOTIONS ARE ARISING FOR YOU?

MOVE IT! GO FOR A RUN, DANCE WITH FRIENDS, PUNCH A PILLOW-

WHAT ARE SOME OF YOUR FAVORITE ACTIVITIES?

IF YOU CAN INCORPORATE THEM INTO YOUR WEEKLY/MONTHLY/YEARLY LIFE— **DO IT! HOW CAN YOU MAKE THAT HAPPEN?**

HAVING SUPPORTIVE ACTIVITIES, PEOPLE, PLACES, AND ITEMS CAN ALL BE HELPFUL STEPS TO NAVIGATING YOUR GRIEF.

LIST SOME THINGS YOU FIND SUPPORTIVE HERE:

ARE YOU FEELING NUMB? CALL A FRIEND, TAKE A WALK, WRITE A POEM: **WHAT SOUNDS LIKE A FIRST STEP FOR YOU?**

WHAT ITEMS SUPPORT YOUR SELF CARE?

WHAT ACTIVITIES SUPPORT YOUR SELF CARE?

WHEN YOU ARE READY- WHAT IS THE WORST F*CKING PART OF THIS LOSS?
DRAW IT OUT, WRITE IT OUT, TALK IT OUT

WHEN YOU ARE READY- WHAT IS THE WORST F*CKING PART OF LIFE WITHOUT THEM?
DRAW IT OUT, WRITE IT OUT, TALK IT OUT

YOU ARE NOT ALONE!

CHECK IN WITH LOVED ONES, FIND A GRIEF GROUP, TALK TO YOUR PETS IF YOU CAN–

EVEN IF IT IS A TEXT OR CALL, HOW CAN YOU KEEP IN TOUCH WITH PEOPLE DURING THIS TIME?

NOTHING CAN REPLACE YOUR LOVED ONE(S), **GRIEVING TAKES TIME.** USE THIS PAGE TO WRITE SELF-AFFIRMATIONS TO YOURSELF

SETTING BOUNDARIES WHEN GRIEVING CAN BE TOUGH.
LET YOUR FRIENDS & LOVED ONES KNOW WHAT YOU NEED, WHAT YOU ARE READY AND NOT TO TALK ABOUT, WHAT PLANS ARE IN PLACE IF YOU NEED SUPPORT.
WHAT ARE SOME THINGS YOU WANT TO SHARE WITH THEM?

LET'S BREATHE:
SET A TIME EACH DAY TO TAKE SOME
DEEP BREATHS
USE THIS PAGE AS YOU WISH

MINDFULNESS MATTERS! GRIEF DOESN'T GO AWAY, IT GETS EASIER TO HOLD OVER TIME. THAT TIME IS THE SPACE YOU ARE GIVING YOUR MIND, BODY, SPIRIT TO PROCESS YOUR GRIEF.

GRIEF CAN TURN YOUR WORLD UPSIDE DOWN WHAT HELPS BRING IT RIGHT SIDE UP?

SOMETIMES WHEN SOMEONE WE LOVE DIES WE HAVE TO TAKE CARE OF THEIR PERSONAL ACCOUNTS. THIS CAN BE OVERWHELMING. MAKING A LIST CAN HELP IT FEEL LESS DAUNTING, AND CHECKING ONE THING OFF AT A TIME IS A MOUNTAIN YOU CLIMBED & SURVIVED

LIST OF CRAP TO TAKE CARE OF:

DO YOU HAVE TO TRAVEL SOMEWHERE FOR YOUR LOSS? **WHAT DOES BEING IN THIS PLACE REMIND YOU OF?**

WHAT **MEMORIES** DO YOU HAVE WITH YOUR LOVED ONE(S) THAT MAKE CERTAIN PLACES HARD TO GO TO?

KEEP YOUR SELF CARE GOING WHILE YOU ARE VISITING

IF YOU EXPERIENCE NEGATIVE/STARTLING MEMORIES CONNECTED TO SPECIFIC PLACES YOU'LL NEED TO GO BACK TO, TRY THIS:

FIND A SMALL OBJECT (EG. BABIES SOCK, PERSONAL ITEM, SENTIMENTAL PIECE, STRESS BALL) AND HOLD IT IN YOUR HAND. FEEL THE ITEM IN YOUR HAND, AND TAKE A FEW DEEP BREATHS. WHAT DO YOU FEEL? WHAT DOES IT HELP YOU THINK ABOUT? THINK ABOUT WHY THAT OBJECT BRINGS YOU TO A CALMER SPACE.

GROUNDING YOURSELF CAN BE HARD DURING GRIEF, UTILIZING IT CAN SUPPORT YOU THROUGH THE THINGS YOU WANT TO GET ACCOMPLISHED WHILE LIVING ON THE GRIEF AXIS OF LIFE.

USE THIS PAGE TO DRAW WHAT FEELINGS YOU ARE PROCESSING

WHEN YOU MISS YOUR LOVED ONE WHAT HELPS YOU FEEL CLOSER TO THEM?

THINK ABOUT A KEEPSAKE, A FRAMED PHOTO IN A VISIBLE AREA, A BOX OF THINGS YOU KEPT FROM YOUR TIME TOGETHER, PRINT OUT TEXTS YOU CARE ABOUT, **THERE ARE SO MANY CREATIVE WAYS TO COMMEMORATE THEM.**

WHAT SONGS MAKE YOU CRY?

WHAT SONGS REMIND YOU OF THE GOOD TIMES WITH YOUR LOVED ONE?

WHAT SONGS HELP YOU FEEL STRONG?

WHAT SONGS ARE ON THE "NO FLY" LIST FOR NOW?
MEANING THEY ARE TOO HARD TO LISTEN TO AFTER THIS LOSS

WHAT IS LEFT UNSAID?

WRITE A POEM, LETTER, SONG, HAIKU, SOMETHING TO EXPRESS THIS:

LET'S TAKE ANOTHER LOOK AT THAT DAILY ROUTINE- WHAT NEEDS TO BE UPDATED, WHAT IS WORKING?

MORNING ROUTINE:

MID-DAY ROUTINE:

NIGHT TIME ROUTINE:

WHAT ARE SOME OF YOUR FAVORITE FOODS?

WHAT WERE SOME OF THEIR FAVORITE FOODS? (IF THEY WEREN'T A PET THEN MAYBE TRY ADDING A DISH THEY LOVED TO A RITUAL FOR THEM)

IF YOU HAVE BEEN A CARETAKER DURING THIS TIME,
WHO TAKES CARE OF YOU?

EVEN IF YOUR NATURE IS TO HELP- EVERYONE NEEDS PEOPLE TO SUPPORT THEM.

WHAT HAS IT BEEN LIKE BEING A CARETAKER? CARETAKING CAN LOOK LIKE TAKING ON PHYSICAL DUTIES, EMOTIONAL DUTIES, AND NEW ROLES.

HAVE YOU HAD DREAMS ABOUT YOUR LOVED ONE? IF SO, WRITE SOME OF THEM HERE:

DREAMS CAN BE SYMBOLIC, HEALING, NIGHTMARISH, AND MANY IN BETWEENS

SOMETIMES IT "DOESN'T HAPPEN" AND IT FEELS LIKE WE ARE DISCONNECTED FROM OUR LOVED ONE. WHAT HAS YOUR EXPERIENCE BEEN?

WHAT ARE SOME WAYS THAT HELP YOU FEEL MORE CONNECTED TO YOUR LOVED ONE?

THERE ARE PEOPLE OUT THERE THAT CAN HELP!
SEARCH FOR LOCAL SUPPORT GROUPS, GRIEF COUNSELORS, HOSPICE SERVICES, PSYCHOTHERAPISTS IF YOU FEEL THAT MAY BE SUPPORTIVE TO YOUR GRIEF. LIST OPTIONS BELOW:

WRITE SOME THINGS YOU WANT TO PROCESS BUT MIGHT NOT BE READY TO:

For the ones experiencing Anticipatory Grief

ANTICIPATORY GRIEF COVERS A WIDE VARIETY OF LOSS.
MAYBE A FRIEND IS BATTLING A LONG TERM ILLNESS, YOUR PET HAS TO BE PUT DOWN, YOU KNOW YOUR RELATIONSHIP IS COMING TO AN END, OR A LOVED ONE LEARNED THAT THEIR TIME IS LIMITED. WHATEVER IT MAY BE- YOUR EMOTIONS ARE YOUR OWN.
PROCESS, TALK, & PLAN ABOUT WHAT YOU WANT TO EXPERIENCE BEFORE THIS END OCCURS.

THERE IS TIME. WHAT WOULD YOU STILL LIKE TO SAY TO YOUR LOVED ONE?

WHAT ACTIVITIES, FOODS, PLACES, AND THINGS WOULD YOU LIKE TO DO WITH THEM BEFORE THEY PASS? IF THEY CANNOT TRAVEL, WHAT ARE CREATIVE WAYS TO DO THESE THINGS?

WHAT IS LEFT UNSAID?

WHAT FEELS HARD TO PROCESS WHILE THERE IS STILL TIME?

ANTICIPATORY GRIEF CAN FEEL DAUNTING, AND OVERPOWERING WITH STRESS & FEARS...
WHAT PROVIDES YOU COMFORT THROUGH THIS TIME?

ARE YOU PLAYING A ROLE IN THEIR LEVEL OF COMFORT BEFORE THE END?
WHAT RITUALS, ITEMS, JOKES, TALKS, THINGS ARE HELPING YOU ALL THROUGH THIS?

HOW HAVE THEY ENRICHED YOUR LIFE?

WHAT ARE SOME OF YOUR FAVORITE MEMORIES WITH YOUR LOVED ONE?

WHAT SELF CARE ITEMS, PEOPLE, AND PLACES DO YOU HAVE AT THE READY FOR WHEN THE TIME COMES?

ARE YOU SLEEPING? SOMETIMES GRIEF AFFECTS OUR SLEEP IN THE FORM OF OVERTHINKING, ANXIETY, DEPRESSION SYMPTOMS- THE LIST GOES ON.
WHEN YOU CAN'T SLEEP- WRITE:

NOTHING CAN FULLY PREPARE YOU THROUGH ANTICIPATORY GRIEF. MAINTAINING A ROUTINE CAN FEEL WEIRD BUT SUPPORTIVE.

MORNING ROUTINE:

MID-DAY ROUTINE:

 **NIGHT TIME ROUTINE:**

INSERT PHOTO OF YOUR LOVED ONE(S) HERE!

HOW CAN YOU STAY CONNECTED?
ANTICIPATORY GRIEF CAN COME WITH A LOT OF DOCTORS VISITS, COUNSELING, TREATMENTS; IT IS IMPORTANT TO FIND WAYS TO STAY CONNECTED TO PEOPLE.

DO YOU FIND SPIRITUAL CONNECTION HELPFUL? IF SO, TRY TO BE CONSISTENT WITH YOUR PRACTICES & COMMUNITY

USE THIS PAGE TO DRAW OUT YOUR
PAINFUL EMOTIONS

WHAT ARE SOME BOUNDARIES YOU WANT TO SET FOR YOURSELF?

HOW CAN YOU TELL PEOPLE WHAT YOU NEED?

MINDFULNESS TOOL:

5 Senses Meditation

Close your eyes if you are comfortable doing so- and name these things:

5 Things You Can See
4 Things You Can Hear
3 Things You Can Feel
2 Things You Can Smell
1 Thing You Can Taste

THIS MINI MINDFULNESS TOOL STEMS FROM A JAPANESE RITUAL CALLED **SHINRIN-YOKU,** OR **FOREST BATHING**/TAKING IN THE ATMOSPHERE.

TAKING A FEW MINUTES TO BE IN THE HERE & NOW, NOT THINKING ABOUT ANYTHING OTHER THAN THESE 5 SENSES AROUND YOU AND IN YOUR BODY CAN HELP RECENTER YOUR MIND.

For the ones experiencing Ambiguous Grief

AMBIGUOUS GRIEF CAN BE TRICKY.

MAYBE A FRIEND GHOSTED YOU, YOUR PARTNER LEFT WITH NO EXPLANATION, OR MAYBE THE CONNECTION YOU HAD WITH A LOVED ONE DOESN'T MEET YOUR EXPECTATIONS. WHATEVER IT MAY BE- YOUR EMOTIONS ARE YOURS TO FEEL. **TALK TO FRIENDS, A PROFESSIONAL, WRITE IT DOWN- TRY TO FIGURE OUT WHAT HURTS ABOUT IT SO YOU CAN HEAL FROM IT.**

WHAT IS FRUSTRATING ABOUT HOW THINGS HAVE GONE?

WHAT OTHER EMOTIONS COME UP FROM THIS CHANGE?

WHAT ARE THE TOP 5 THINGS YOU WANT FROM A CONNECTION (FRIENDSHIP, RELATIONSHIP, FAMILY DYNAMIC) **THAT WASN'T ADDRESSED IN THAT PREVIOUS CONNECTION?**

DO YOU FEEL YOU DESERVE THE THINGS YOU JUST LISTED?

WHAT ARE SOME THINGS THAT THIS PERSON IS MISSING OUT ON NOW THAT YOU AREN'T IN THEIR LIFE?

WHAT ELSE IS AWESOME ABOUT YOU?

HOW CAN YOU PROTECT YOUR PEACE?

SOMETIMES AMBIGUOUS GRIEF IS ON GOING, IF THAT IS THE CASE, **HOW COULD YOU GET TO A SPACE OF RESOLUTION OR CLOSURE** IF SOMEONE ELSE CAN'T PROVIDE THAT FOR YOU?

YOUR EXPERIENCE IS VALID. JUST BECAUSE THE PERSON IS STILL ALIVE, DOESN'T MEAN IT DOESN'T HURT LIKE A MOFO.

HAS ANYONE AROUND YOU EXPERIENCED A SIMILAR SITUATION? **TALK IT OUT!** WHAT WOULD YOU LIKE TO SHARE WITH THEM?

IF YOU COULD HAVE CLOSURE WITH THIS, WHAT WOULD YOU WANT TO SAY?

AFTER YOU WRITE IT DOWN, THINK ABOUT IT- AND RIP THIS PAGE OUT!

WHAT DID YOU LIKE ABOUT WHO YOU WERE BEFORE THIS HAPPENED?

WHAT DID YOU NOT LIKE ABOUT YOURSELF BEFORE THIS HAPPENED?

IT'S OK TO LIKE AND DISLIKE PARTS OF YOURSELF FOR A LITTLE WHILE, IT HELPS US GAGE HOW **WE CAN GROW INTO THE PEOPLE WE WANT TO BE.**

WHAT IS HARD TO LET GO FROM THIS EXPERIENCE?

WHAT'S SOMETHING YOU'VE LEARNED FROM THIS EXPERIENCE? (IF APPLICABLE)

TALKING TO AN OUTSIDE PERSPECTIVE
CAN HELP YOU HEAL.
WHO CAN BE THAT SUPPORT FOR YOU?

**WHAT DO YOU THINK
CAN HELP YOU HEAL?**

YOU ARE IMPORTANT, SMART, LOVED, & SO MUCH MORE.

WHAT THINGS IN LIFE AFFIRM THIS STATEMENT IS TRUE FOR YOU?

IF YOU DON'T BELIEVE IT YET, THINK ABOUT TALKING TO A PROFESSIONAL TO DEVELOP YOUR SELF LOVE.

WHAT ARE YOU PROUD OF YOURSELF FOR?

WRITE 3 AFFIRMATIONS YOU CAN SAY OR WRITE EACH DAY:

_____

_____

_____

_____

_____

FINDING FUN HOBBIES IS A GOOD
STRESS RELIEVER

WRITE A SHORT STORY:

OR BE REBELLIOUS AND DRAW A STORY

For the ones experiencing Complicated Grief

COMPLICATED GRIEF CAN FEEL STRENUOUS.
THE DEFINITION INVOLVES SYMPTOMS BEING LONGER "THAN USUAL". BUT **WHAT IS "USUAL" ABOUT LOSS?** IF YOU ARE EXPERIENCING SYMPTOMS WHERE YOU CANNOT FUNCTION IN DAILY LIFE OVER DAYS, WEEKS, MONTHS- IT'S TIME TO MAKE A PROFESSIONAL CONNECTION WITH A THERAPIST. IF YOU FEEL PRESSURED THAT YOU'RE STILL GRIEVING AFTER A LONG PERIOD OF TIME- MAYBE IT'S BECAUSE **GRIEF F*CKING SUCKS.**

TAKE A SECOND TO BREATHE DEEPLY

INHALE THROUGH YOUR NOSE

5
4
3
2
1

EXHALE THROUGH YOUR MOUTH

5
4
3
2
1

DO THIS A FEW TIMES TO RECONNECT WITH YOUR BODY & CALM YOUR NERVOUS SYSTEM

SO YOU'RE GRIEVING... AND EVERYTHING STILL SUCKS.
TAKE IT ONE STEP AT A TIME. WRITE SOME OF THOSE STEPS BELOW:

MAKE A LIST: WHAT ARE THE BASIC THINGS, AS A HUMAN BEING, I NEED TO DO? (EAT, SLEEP, TAKE A BATH/SHOWER, MAYBE BRUSH MY HAIR)

WHO DO YOU KNOW THAT CAN HELP?
WHAT LOCAL SERVICES MAY BE AVAILABLE FOR YOU?

WHAT TYPE OF CHECK INS OR REMINDERS CAN YOU MAKE TO KEEP IN CONTACT WITH OTHERS?

EVEN IF YOU SNOOZE YOUR ALARM, OR WANT TO BE ALONE SOMETIMES, KEEP THESE THINGS IN MIND

WHAT'S FEELING HARD TO HOLD ABOUT THIS LOSS?

HAVE YOU LET YOURSELF FEEL THESE FEELINGS?
IF NOT, WHAT IS HOLDING YOU BACK FROM PROCESSING THIS?

**IT IS OKAY THAT IT STILL HURTS LIKE A MOFO.
GRIEF DOESN'T MAGICALLY GO AWAY, WE LEARN TO LIVE WITH IT.
IF YOUR GRIEF COULD TAKE A "FORM" (EG. MYTHICAL CREATURE, SHARK, SPLINTER, ETC) DRAW WHAT IT WOULD LOOK LIKE HERE:**

ARE YOU CRITICIZING YOUR OWN EXPERIENCE?

IF SO, **WHAT IS UNDERLYING THOSE FEELINGS** OF REGRET, SURVIVORS GUILT, SHAME, OR WHATEVER ELSE IT MAY BE?

WHAT IS WITHIN YOUR POWER TO HELP YOURSELF FIND ACCEPTANCE OF YOUR LOVED ONES DEATH? (E.G. HAVE PHOTOS OF THEM AROUND THE HOUSE, GO VISIT THEIR BURIEL SITE, TALK TO THEM OUT LOUD...)

HI

WRITE A LETTER TO YOUR LOVED ONE(S) YOU LOST:

WRITE A LETTER TO YOURSELF, AS IF YOU ARE A FRIEND TO YOURSELF:

WHAT MUSIC HELPS YOU PROCESS YOUR EMOTIONS?

WHAT TV SHOWS OR MOVIES HELP YOU PROCESS YOUR EMOTIONS?

WHAT ACTIVITIES HELP YOU PROCESS YOUR EMOTIONS? (EG. RUNNING, PAINTING, KNITTING, YOGA, DANCING)

ARE YOU SICK OF THE WORD PROCESS YET?
SAME

WHAT IS A PART OF YOURSELF YOU HAVE LOST FROM THIS GRIEF?

MAYBE A PIECE OF US LEAVES, BUT IT WAS THERE IN THE FIRST PLACE BECAUSE OF OUR EXPERIENCE, RELATIONSHIP, PET OR PERSON WE LOVE.

**HOW HAVE YOU CHANGED FROM
THE START OF THIS JOURNAL TO NOW?**

**WHAT ARE SOME OF YOUR HOPES FOR
YOUR FUTURE SELF?**

For the ones experiencing Collective Grief

COLLECTIVE GRIEF IS MULTIFACETED. ALL GRIEF IS MULTIFACETED BUT COLLECTIVE GRIEF CREATES SHARED MEANING OF WHAT HAS HAPPENED AS WELL AS TRYING TO FIND SPACE FOR HOW YOU FEEL ABOUT WHAT HAS HAPPENED. **EVERYONE HAS THEIR OWN WAY OF PROCESSING,** AND WHILE COMMUNITY SUPPORT IN A TRYING TIME IS HELPFUL, **MAKING SURE YOU ARE VALIDATING YOUR PERSONAL EXPERIENCE IS IMPORTANT TOO.**

IF THIS IS A COMMUNITY LOSS, WHAT RITUALS ARE BEING COORDINATED TO PAY TRIBUTE TO THIS LIFE (OR LIVES)?

WHAT ROLE CAN YOU PLAY IN THESE RITUALS THAT FEELS SUPPORTIVE AND HEALING TO YOU?

IF THIS LOSS HAS BEEN ABRUPT, WHAT FEELINGS ARE COMING UP FOR YOU, NOW THAT YOU KNOW WHAT HAS HAPPENED?

DO YOU FEEL SUPPORTED BY YOUR COMMUNITY?

IF NOT, WHO IS YOUR CHOSEN COMMUNITY?

WHAT MIGHT STOP YOU FROM FULLY EXPRESSING YOUR EMOTIONS?

ARE THESE REASONS BASED ON IDEALIZED VIEWS OF HOW YOU "SHOULD" ACT? OR ARE YOU YOUR OWN BARRIER?

COMMUNITY LOSS CAN BE A WIDE SCOPE OF THINGS, FROM NATURAL DISASTERS TO INJUSTICES COMPOUNDED OVER GENERATIONS.

WHAT IS SOMETHING THAT IS REALLY HARD TO PROCESS ABOUT THIS?

WHAT IS SOMETHING THAT MAY SUPPORT YOUR OWN PROCESS OF HEALING?

WHAT MIGHT HELP YOU SUPPORT YOUR COMMUNITY'S HEALING?

ARE THERE LASTING RITUALS (EG. MEMORIALS, TOWN MEETINGS, FACEBOOK GROUPS, RELIGIOUS RITUALS, CONNECTIONS) **FOR YOU TO CONNECT WITH THE PEOPLE WHO ALSO WENT THROUGH THIS?**

IS CONNECTION TO THIS GROUP HEALING OR HARMFUL TO YOUR OWN PROCESS RIGHT NOW?

WHAT IS YOUR VIEW OF TALKING TO A MENTAL HEALTH PROFESSIONAL?

IF IT IS A POSITIVE VIEW, WHAT STEPS CAN YOU TAKE TO TALK TO A MENTAL HEALTH PROFESSIONAL?

IF IT IS A LESS POSITIVE VIEW, WHAT ALTERNATIVES ARE THERE FOR SUPPORTING YOUR MENTAL HEALTH?

Questions to think of when searching for a Therapist:

- Are they in your area? Try to search locally or in your state.
- Does their rate per session match with your budget?
- Are they offering the service you are looking for? Some therapists are specialized in certain trainings for specific presenting problems.
- Do they accept your insurance? (if applicable)
- What are their credentials?
- Check their vibe- Do they seem like someone you could form a therapeutic relationship with?
- Do you want someone with specific demographics?
- Do you prefer tele-therapy or in-person sessions?
- Are you ready to commit to therapy?

WHAT DO YOU APPRECIATE ABOUT YOUR COMMUNITY DURING THIS COLLECTIVE GRIEF?

IF THE COLLECTIVE GRIEF IS TRIGGERING (EG. POSTERS, VIGILS, GATHERINGS) CHECK IN WITH YOURSELF; TAKING TIME & SPACE FOR YOURSELF IS VALID.

USE THIS PAGE TO HONOR THIS LOSS.

IF THERE IS A VIGIL OR FORM OF OFFERING RITUAL, USE THIS PAGE TO WRITE A LETTER:

DO YOU HAVE DREAMS OF YOUR LOVED ONE(S) WHO HAVE DIED?

WRITE ABOUT THE DREAMS HERE & IN THE BLANK PAGES IF YOU WISH.
DREAM MAPPING OR JOURNALING CAN FEEL SUPPORTIVE DURING HEALING

SOMETIMES LIFE SUCKS.
SOMETIMES WE ARE JUST **STUCK
AND THAT IS OKAY**.
HEALING TAKES TIME. BUT ARE WE EVER
FULLY HEALED? MAYBE NOT- BUT I LIKE
TO THINK THE PEOPLE, PLACES,
THINGS THAT BRING US JOY &
COMFORT US--
**THESE THINGS ARE ESSENTIAL TO
KEEP ON GOING.**

GRIEF MEMORY BOX:

FIND ITEMS YOU HAVE FROM YOUR LOVED ONE, RELATIONSHIP, PET, OR EVENT YOU ARE GRIEVING.

PUT ITEMS IN A BOX, AND WRITE OR COVER THE BOX IN LOVING WORDS, PHOTOS, COLLAGE ART AND OTHER MEDIUMS OF CREATION.

PLACE THE BOX SOMEWHERE SAFE & REMEMBER THAT IT IS ALWAYS THERE FOR YOU TO VISIT WHEN YOU ARE READY TO LOOK THROUGH IT AND WALK THROUGH YOUR MEMORIES.

FUTURE PROMPTS:

- HOW HAVE I CHANGED SINCE I LAST WROTE IN THIS JOURNAL?
- WHAT DO I APPRECIATE ABOUT WHAT I HAVE GOTTEN THROUGH?
- AM I PROUD OF WHERE I AM NOW?
- WHO HAS TURNED OUT TO BE A SUPPORTIVE PERSON IN MY GRIEF JOURNEY?
- WHAT HAS SURPRISED ME ABOUT THE TIME THAT HAS PASSED SINCE MY GRIEF BEGAN?
- WHAT IS MY MENTAL HEALTH LIKE NOW?
- AM I GETTING THE SUPPORT I NEED?
- WHAT ARE MY HOPES FOR MY FUTURE SELF?
- WHAT EMOTIONS COME UP WHEN I THINK OF MY LOVED ONE NOW THAT I HAVE HAD MORE TIME?

MINI SAFETY PLAN:

1. **WHEN DO I KNOW IT'S TIME TO IMPLEMENT THE SAFETY PLAN?** (WHEN MY EMOTIONS ARE HARD TO HOLD ALONE, FEELINGS OF SELF HARM, FEELING HOPELESSNESS, ETC.):

2. **WHAT COPING SKILLS DO I HAVE?** (GOING FOR A WALK, TV SHOWS, BOOKS, FRIENDS, ART, EXERCISE, ETC)

3. **WHO CAN I CALL WHEN I'M IN CRISIS?**
    I. **NAME:**
    II. **PHONE #:**
    III. **NAME:**
    IV. **PHONE #:**

4. **WHAT AGENCIES CAN I CONTACT IN A CRISIS?**
    I. **LOCAL HOSPITAL:**
    II. **URGENT CARE:**
    III. **THERAPIST:**
    IV. **SUICIDE PREVENTION LIFELINE PHONE: 1-800-273-TALK (8255)**

5. **WHAT DO I NEED TO DO TO MAKE MY ENVIRONMENT SAFE? LEAVE? GET RID OF WEAPONS? TALK TO FRIENDS TO NOT BE ISOLATED?**

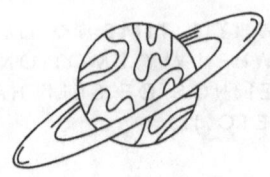

GRIEF DOES NOT END AFTER FINISHING THIS JOURNAL.

THIS IS JUST THE BEGINNING OF GETTING TO KNOW YOURSELF, YOUR HEALING TOOLS, AND YOUR SUPPORT SYSTEM BETTER.

WHEN I HAVE FACED MY OWN GRIEF, THESE HAVE BEEN QUESTIONS I HAVE ASKED MYSELF, AND I HOPE THAT THEY ARE HELPFUL REFLECTIONS FOR YOU AS WELL.

MY GRIEF TAUGHT ME THAT WE ARE NEVER TRULY ALONE, EVEN WHEN IT FEELS LIKE WE ARE IN OUR OWN UNIVERSE SOMEWHERE FAR AWAY ON *PLANET GRIEF*.

IF THESE EMOTIONS & THOUGHTS EVER GET TOO HARD TO HOLD, REACH OUT TO A MENTAL HEALTH PROFESSIONAL, A FRIEND, A LOVED ONE, A TRUSTED PERSON, A CRISIS HOTLINE- AND GET THE SUPPORT YOU NEED!!!

MY HEART GOES OUT TO EACH PERSON OUT THERE EXPERIENCING A FORM OF GRIEF.

SIMONE EBRIGHT

ABOUT THE AUTHOR

Simone Ebright is a grief survivor who took her experiences and turned them into a career. She received her Master's Degree in Couples & Family Therapy from Seattle University in 2021 and is currently a Licensed Marriage and Family Therapist Associate in Washington. She is the CEO of Koger Counseling which is a private tele-therapy practice in Washington state.

Her journal, Grief F*cking Sucks is the first in a series of healing tools to support people experiencing different forms of grief.

Find more information on her business profiles:
Blog: Walks with Simone
Instagram: @kogercounseling
www.kogercounseling.com

You are not alone. ✨

www.ingramcontent.com/pod-product-compliance
Lightning Source LLC
Chambersburg PA
CBHW071742150426
43191CB00010B/1655